My First Book of Bible Stories

CONTENTS

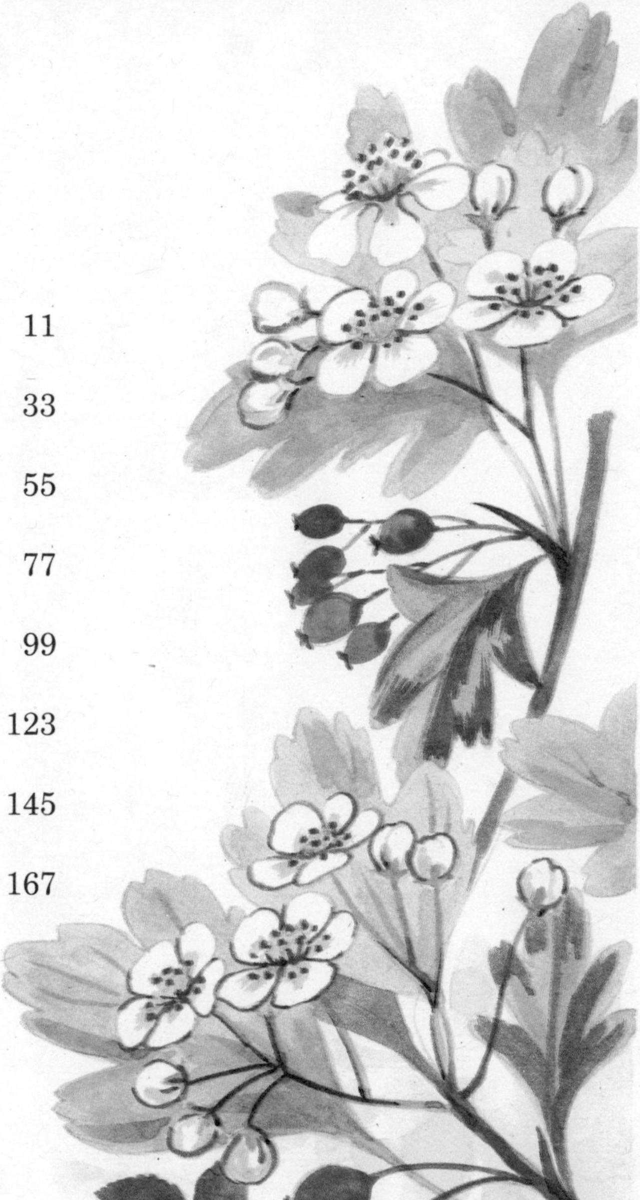

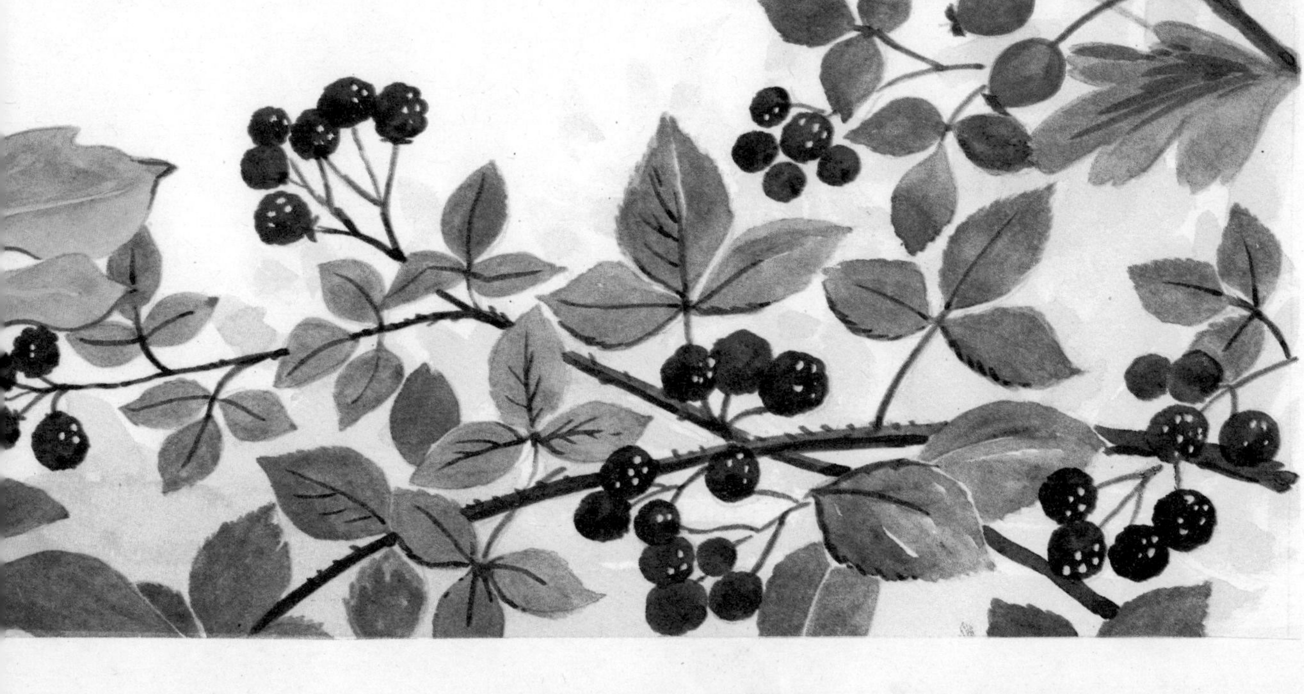

Printed in the USSR for the publisher Peter Haddock Ltd., Bridlington

Stories from
THE OLD TESTAMENT

THE CREATION

A long time ago, before the world was even made, there was God. God has always been there and always will be. There has never been a time without Him.

12

It was God who made the world and everything in it, and nothing can live, breathe or grow without Him. In the beginning, everywhere was dark and covered by water. Nothing had any shape.

But God's power and spirit were there. When God said, 'Let there be light', there was light. He divided the light from the dark, and called the light Day and the darkness Night.

14

On the second day, God shaped the sky like a great
dome between the waters above and the waters below.

16

Then the next day, He gathered the waters below together and called them the Sea. The dry land which was left He called the Earth. Here He planted grass and seeds and trees and all kinds of plants. Some of them grew grain and some grew fruit. As they grew they dropped seeds, full of new life. In time these seeds grew into new trees and plants; and so living things have gone on growing ever since.

On the fourth day, God created the Sun and the Moon to give light and to mark the passing of day into night. So, since then, there have been days and seasons and years. And He made the twinkling stars which shine so prettily at night.

Everything looked very beautiful and God was pleased with His work.

The day afterwards, He decided to make fish and birds. All kinds of fish were given to the Earth's waters — from giant sea-monsters down to tiny little fish, which can hardly be seen.

He filled the sky with winged creatures of every kind — big birds, tiny ones, bats, butterflies, moths, flying insects, and thousands more.

God gave all these creatures life, so that they too could grow and have families. This is why they are still with us today. It is God's power which created the world and which enables it to live on.

On the sixth day, God created all sorts of animals — large and small, wild and tame. There were elephants, rhinos, kangaroos and giraffes. There were snakes, horses, bears, cows, sheep and goats. And there were

dogs, cats, rabbits, hedgehogs, hamsters, mice and many, many more. Every creature was perfectly formed and wonderfully made.

But God knew that all these living things would need to be cared for. So He created Man and Woman. First He made a man and called him Adam. Then He gave him a wife, who was named Eve. God wanted them to be happy together, so He gave them a beautiful garden for a home. This was the Garden of Eden.

24

He told them that they could eat any fruits they liked, except for one special fruit which they must never eat. If they did, then things would go very wrong.

On the seventh day God rested, for now His world was complete. He blessed this day and made it a very special day indeed. And that is why we have one day in seven when we rest from our work and prepare ourselves for the week ahead. But, more important, this is the day when we give our thanks to God for all that He has done for us.

Sadly, God's world did not stay as beautiful as He wanted it to be.

One day, a cunning snake told Eve that she could eat the fruit from the forbidden tree. So she did just that.

   Then she gave some to Adam and he ate it too.

As soon as they had swallowed it, they remembered God's words and knew they had done wrong. They were sad and sorry.

God was sorry too, for they had spoilt His world by doing wrong.

He said to them, 'Because you disobeyed me, you will have to leave the Garden of Eden. You will always have to work hard to make the land produce food.'

29

So He sent them out of the beautiful garden, and sin and sadness came into the world.

But later in the Bible we see how sin and sadness can be beaten. No one can ever overcome the wonderful power of God.

30

Jesus came into the world to show us how God's love can help us to deal with the wrong and bad things in life. If we try and live like Jesus, we can help to make the world as beautiful as God intended it to be.

THE FALL OF JERICHO

Moses was a great leader and, when he died, God chose a new leader named Joshua.

'You must be very brave and strong,' God told Joshua. 'I will be with you, just as I was with Moses.' So Joshua set off to lead the Israelites, who had nearly reached the land which God had promised them many years ago.

But two things stood in their way before they could enter the promised land. One was the River Jordan, which they would have to cross; the second was the city of Jericho.

Joshua wanted to know what Jericho was really like, so he sent two spies to explore the city. They stayed for the night at the house of a woman named Rahab. Her house was built into the city wall.

But the King of Jericho heard about the men. He sent messengers to Rahab saying, 'Those men in your house have come to spy! Send them away!'

Now Rahab wanted to protect the men, and she had
hidden them up on the flat roof of her house.
She told the King's messengers that the men had left

at sunset, before the city gate was closed. She said that if the messengers hurried they might catch them. The King's men hurried off to look.

Meanwhile, Rahab went up onto the roof and said to the men, 'I know that the Lord God has given you this land. We have all heard of the wonderful things He has done for you. Your God is God in heaven above and here on earth. Please treat me and my family with kindness when you attack the city, just as I have treated you.'

The men promised and told Rahab that when the city was attacked, she should tie a red cord to her window; then the Israelites would know it was her house and would not harm anyone there.

Rahab agreed and helped the men climb through the window and down the side of the city wall using a rope. Then they went and hid in the hills until the King's men had stopped looking for them.

43

Next, God told Joshua how they were to cross the River Jordan. The priests were to carry the Covenant Box. This had the Ten Commandments inside it and was a sign that God was with them. They were to carry this up to the river's edge, step in the water and stand near the bank.

As soon as they did this, the river stopped flowing.

44

The waters divided and piled up like a great wall on either side. The people were amazed. Now they could actually walk through the river. Nothing is too hard for God to do.

Joshua ordered the men to take twelve stones out of the river and set them on the bank. They would remind people of what God had done for them.

45

Only the city of Jericho now stood in their way. It had high walls around it and the gates were kept shut and guarded.

The Israelites wondered how they could get inside. But God had a plan.

He said to Joshua, 'You and your soldiers must march all round the outside of the city for six days — once every day. In front of you will walk seven priests, each with a trumpet, and they will carry the Covenant Box.'

Then God said, 'On the seventh day, you must march around the city seven times while the priests blow their trumpets. When they sound one long note, everybody must give a loud shout.'

Joshua called the priests together and told them what God had said.

On the first day they went round the city once. The next day they did the same and continued for six days.

On the seventh day they got up at dawn and began their long march, seven times around the city.

The seventh time round, just as the priests were
about to sound their trumpets, Joshua ordered, 'Shout!
The Lord has given you the city!'
Everybody gave a great shout and the walls of
Jericho came crashing down!

The Israelites rushed into the city and captured Jericho.

51

Joshua had told them that they were not to take anything, but any silver, gold, bronze or iron was to be set apart and given to the Lord.

Rahab's family were saved, because the Israelites saw the red cord in her window. She had shown the spies that she believed in God.

Joshua became famous throughout the land as a great leader and a true servant of God. The people knew that God was with him; they had seen the wonderful things which could happen when God was on their side. Joshua told the people, 'Decide today whom you will serve. As for me and my family, we will serve the Lord.'

RUTH
& NAOMI

A long time ago, in Bethlehem, there lived a lady named Naomi. She had a husband named Elimelech and two grown-up sons and they all lived happily together.

A time came when the crop failed and they hardly had anything to eat. Naomi and her family decided to

move to another country, called Moab. It was a long
way away, on the other side of the Dead Sea. The
family put all they needed into a bag and set off for
their new life.

They arrived in Moab at last and settled there. When they had been there some time, Elimelech died. Naomi was very sad. Now she had only her two sons. She was happy when they both married girls from Moab. One of the wives was named Orpah and the other was named Ruth.

For about ten years they all lived happily. There was food to eat and work to do. But then came more sadness. The two sons died. Now only Naomi, Orpah and Ruth were left.

'I will go back to my old home,' said Naomi. 'I hear there has been a good harvest and there is food to eat there now.'

Orpah and Ruth loved Naomi very much. They set off with her, although they did not come from Naomi's country. Naomi wanted Orpah and Ruth to be happy, but she thought they would be happier in their own country.

'Go back to your own mothers,' she said. 'You have been very kind to me. May God be kind to you too. He may want you to marry again and have children.'

60

Orpah and Ruth did not want to leave Naomi, loving her as they did. They both started to cry. Naomi said, 'It would be much better for you to stay in your own country, with your own people.'

Finally, Orpah decided that Naomi was right. She kissed her goodbye and set off for home.

But Ruth held onto Naomi. 'Do not ask me to leave you,' she said. 'I love you. Let me go with you. Where you live, I want to live too.'

Naomi knew that Ruth would not change her mind, so she said no more and let Ruth go with her.

It was a long walk back to Bethlehem. When they arrived everyone was very pleased to see Naomi again. Ruth felt that she must go out and work, so that she and Naomi would both have enough to eat. It was the time of the barley harvest. In those days, farmers used to leave some grain growing round the edges of the fields, so that the poor people might come and

gather it. It was a kind thing to do and it was called 'gleaning'. This is what Ruth did.

She worked in the field of a good man named Boaz. During the day, he came to the field to see how the work was coming on. When he noticed Ruth, he asked the man in charge who she was, for he had not seen her before.

'She came back from Moab with Naomi,' the man replied. 'She has been working hard all day. Only now has she stopped to rest.' He told Boaz how good Ruth had been to Naomi.

Boaz went over to Ruth. 'You can always work in this

field,' he said to her. 'Stay with the women here. I have asked the men to treat you kindly. When you are thirsty, go and drink from the water jars which they have filled.'

Ruth was surprised. 'Why are you so kind to me?' she asked, bowing down. 'I am a foreigner.'

'I have heard how kind you were to Naomi,' replied Boaz. 'You would not leave her to come back here alone.'

At mealtimes Boaz asked Ruth to come and share the food. When she went back to work, Boaz asked his men to leave some extra corn for her to pick up. That evening, when Ruth got home, she told Naomi about it.

Naomi was very surprised. 'Boaz is one of our relatives!' she exclaimed.

Each day Ruth went to work in the field until all the

crop had been gathered. She came to know Boaz very well.

In those days, if a man died leaving no children, his brother or the next nearest relative had to marry the widow so that the family could be continued. He also had to buy the dead man's land so that it could be kept in the family.

Although Boaz was a relation of Ruth's by marriage, there was another man who was an even closer relation to Ruth.

So Boaz said to Ruth, 'Tomorrow we will find out if that relative of yours will look after you and marry you. If he won't, then I will.'

70

The next day, Boaz went up to the town gate where he knew he would see Ruth's nearest relation. Lots of important business took place at the town gate, where there were many people to see that promises were kept.

Boaz waited, and when the man came by, Boaz said, 'Come over here, my friend, and sit down.' They talked and it was agreed that Boaz should marry Ruth.

Then Boaz asked ten of the leaders of the town to sit down with them. He asked the relative if he would like to buy the field which had belonged to Elimelech. 'I will buy it,' agreed the man.
'Then you must also marry Ruth,' said Boaz, 'And the field will stay in Elimelech's family.'

This did not please the man. He thought it would mean that his own children would be left out if the field went into Ruth's family for her future children. So he said he would not buy the field after all. 'You buy it,' he said to Boaz.

He then took off one of his sandals and gave it to Boaz. In those days this was a sign that the matter was settled.

Boaz looked around at the ten leaders and the other people who were there. 'You have all seen today that I have bought Elimelech's field from Naomi, and that I will marry Ruth,' he said. The leaders all agreed

74

and gave him their good wishes.

So Boaz married Ruth and in due time they had a
baby son. Naomi was thrilled to have a grandson! She
picked him up and held him close.

Years later, when he had grown up Ruth's son had a
grandson of his own who became the great King
David.

DANIEL

There was once a King named Darius, who chose
Daniel, a Jew, to help him look after his country. The
King was so pleased with Daniel's good work that he
decided to put him in charge of his Kingdom. Daniel
asked God for His help.
Kneeling by his window, he prayed to God three
times a day.

The other governors of the Kingdom were jealous of Daniel but they could find nothing wrong with his work. Knowing of Daniel's love of God, they tried to use Him to cause trouble for Daniel.

They asked King Darius to make a new law which said that for 30 days people could only go to the King for advice. No one could ask God for His help. Anyone who did, would be thrown into a den of lions.
The King was pleased and agreed to sign the new law.

Daniel felt that it was more important to obey God than the King, and he went on praying to God as he had before.

But the other men saw him and told the King.

The King was unhappy because he liked Daniel and did not want to lose him. But he had to obey laws just like anyone else.

Sadly, he ordered that Daniel should be arrested and thrown to the lions.

'May your God save you,' he said.

Daniel was thrown into the pit and a big stone was placed over the entrance.

The King returned to his palace feeling very miserable. He could not eat or sleep. He wished now that he had not signed the new law.

The next morning, as soon as it was light, the King hurried to the pit. When he got there he called out, 'Daniel! Did your God save you?'

To his delight, Daniel replied, 'Yes, your majesty. God sent an angel to close the lions' mouths. They did not harm me.'

King Darius was overjoyed. He ordered that Daniel should be pulled out of the pit at once. Then everyone saw that he was not hurt at all.

So the King made yet another new law, which said that everyone must worship Daniel's God.

'God is a living God,' said Darius. 'He will rule for ever.'

Daniel's Three Friends and the Fiery Furnace
(Daniel, chapter 3)

One day, King Nebuchadnezzar made a huge golden statue. It could not move, or speak, or do anything at all, but the King thought it was wonderful.

He told everyone that when they heard the sound of

trumpets and other instruments, they must bow down to the statue. If they did not, they would be thrown into a burning, fiery furnace.

The people did as their King asked. But three of Daniel's friends — Shadrach, Meshach and Abednego — disobeyed him. They would not worship a false god. They wanted to worship the one true God, who they knew was real, and they took no notice of the King's command.

Some cunning men saw this and told the King, who was furious.

'Bring them to me,' he ordered. When the three men came, he said, 'I will give you one more chance. Bow down to the statue now or you will be thrown into the furnace. Can any God save you then?'

The three friends replied, 'We serve the true God, who can save us from the fire and from you. But even if that was not so, we still would not worship the golden statue.'

This made the King even more angry. 'Throw them into the fire,' he raged, 'and make it seven times hotter than usual.'

The strongest men in the army tied up the three
friends and threw them into the fire as the King
watched.

Suddenly, he jumped up. 'Did we not throw three men into the fire? I can see four and they do not seem to be hurt at all.'

The fourth person was perhaps an angel, but the King did not realize this.

He went as close to the furnace as he could and called out to the men, 'Come out! You who serve the true God!'

Shadrach, Meshach and Abednego walked out, not hurt at all.

The flames had not touched them or their clothes and they did not even smell of smoke.

'Praise to their God!' cried the King. 'He sent His angel to rescue these men who serve and trust Him. They risked their lives rather than obey my orders.

Now I command that no one must speak against God ever again. No other God can protect His servants as He does.'

Then he gave Shadrach, Meshach and Abednego important positions in his Kingdom.

JONAH

One day, God sent a message to a prophet named Jonah. He asked him to go to the big city of Nineveh. He was to tell the people there that they would be punished for being so wicked.

100

But Jonah was afraid to go to such a wicked place.
Instead, he boarded a ship sailing in the other
direction, towards Tarshish.

Soon after the ship set sail, a great storm began to blow. The winds were strong and fierce and the ship was tossed about in the rough seas. The sailors were terrified that they would drown. They each prayed to their own gods to help them.

'Our ship will break up!' they cried. They threw out some of the ship's cargo to make it lighter.

Still the storm raged on. Jonah had gone down into the hold, in the bottom of the ship. He had fallen fast asleep.

The captain found him there and woke him up. 'Why have you gone to sleep?' he asked. 'Get up and ask your God to help us. He might feel sorry for us and save us.'

Still the storm blew on. The sailors thought that someone on the ship was to blame. They decided it must be Jonah's fault.

'Who are you?' they asked. 'Where do you come from? Is this storm your fault?'

Jonah told them that he was a Hebrew. He said that his God had made the land and the sea and that he was now punishing Jonah for not doing as he had asked. The storm was Jonah's punishment for not obeying God.

The sailors agreed that Jonah had done wrong.

Jonah suggested that if they threw him overboard the sea might calm down.

At first the sailors would not agree to this. They tried rowing harder and harder instead. But still they could

not reach the land. So they decided to throw Jonah into the sea. They prayed to God to ask Him not to punish them for what they were doing.

Then they threw Jonah into the raging waters. At once the sea calmed down. But poor Jonah! The seawater got into his mouth and he was covered with seaweed. He felt very miserable and thought he was going to die.

The sailors were frightened because of what they had done and promised that they would only serve the true God — Jonah's God.

Jonah swam around, wondering how long he could last. Suddenly a huge fish swam up and swallowed Jonah whole! He was inside the fish for three days and three nights.

This gave him time to think and he knew that he had been wrong to disobey God. He prayed to God, to say he was sorry.

All this time the fish was swimming towards the shore. When it got there it gave a great cough and out popped Jonah!

When Jonah recovered his breath, he heard God speaking to him again. He was giving Jonah another chance.

'Go to Nineveh as I asked you,' He said.

This time Jonah did as God wanted. When he arrived in Nineveh, he cried out that the city would be destroyed because the people were so wicked.
When the people heard this they were truly sorry. They decided that everyone in the land should give up eating and drinking as their punishment. They would also pray to God for His forgiveness. Even the King joined in and ordered everyone to give up their wicked ways.

God saw that the people of Nineveh were really sorry. They were going to try to be better. So He said that He would not punish them by destroying the city. God is always merciful and loving. He always forgives those who are truly sorry and want to do better.

But Jonah was cross about this. He felt that as he had come a long way to deliver God's message, the city should be destroyed. So he went outside the city, where he made a shelter for himself. He sat and sulked. God made a plant grow to give Jonah more shade.

Jonah liked it, but next day a worm ate it. Jonah was angry again.

'Why are you so angry?' asked God. 'Although you did not make the plant grow, you feel sorry for it.'

Jonah agreed.

'So why should I not feel sorry for the people of Nineveh and forgive them?' said God. 'There are thousands of small children living there, and animals.' God was showing Jonah that it is right to show love and mercy. God would much rather forgive people than punish them.

This is how God wanted Jonah, and us, to behave.

Stories from
THE NEW
TESTAMENT

THE SERMON ON THE MOUNT

People loved to listen to Jesus. He told such wonderful stories. So wonderful, they have been remembered ever since.

Once he told a story about two men who each wanted to build a house. First of all, they looked around for a good place to build. The first man found a very good

place, for when he began to dig down, underneath the soil there was solid rock. It was very firm and soon he had built himself a very fine house. He was a wise man.

The second man did not think it important that the walls should be built on solid ground. He decided to build his house on sand. It looked nice too, but, as we shall see, this man was very foolish.

Both men soon finished their work and everyone had to agree that the houses did look very nice. The two builders were very pleased with what they had done. The houses looked strong and sturdy and the men felt

sure that they would last for a very long time. The men thought they had good reason to be proud of themselves.

While the sun shone, the houses did indeed look very beautiful. But one day there was a terrible storm. The rain came flooding down and it raged and beat upon the walls of the houses. Soon the land was flooded with water. The winds tore at everything — trees,

plants, people and buildings. The two men wondered whether their new buildings would ever survive. One of them did.

The house which was built upon rock was the one which stood through the storm. Nothing could shake it, because it had a very firm foundation. Foundations are very important. You cannot see them because they are underground. But it is the foundation which

gives a building its strength. If the foundation is weak, then the whole building is weak too. Sand is a very weak foundation for any building. As soon as the storm hit the house built on sand, it began to collapse.

The storm did not rage for long before this house fell down. It came down with a terrible crash. It crashed because its foundations were weak. The wind and rain soon moved the sand and the house had no support.

After telling this story, Jesus said 'Listen to me and
my teaching. Live the way I live. Then, no matter
what happens to you in life, you will be strong. Your
life will have a firm foundation.'

Jesus also told another story about two men. One looked at the other and said 'Please let me take that little speck out of your eye.'
But he could hardly see to do it, because he had a big log in his own eye! Jesus said 'First he must take the log out of his own eye, then he will be able to

see clearly to remove the speck from the other man's eye.'

By this Jesus meant that we must not always look for the wrong things that other people do, when we do worse things ourselves.

Jesus spoke a great deal about people who loved money, fine clothes, jewels and other riches more than anything else. They buy as many things as they can, but often they find that these things don't last. Perhaps they go rusty, or moths get at the clothes, or thieves come and take everything away.

Jesus called such things 'treasures on earth'. Instead, He said, we should collect 'treasures in heaven', for these are things which can never be taken from us.

Such things as a kind, loving heart; lips which speak only what is good and true; eyes which look where help is needed; and a mind ready to think the best of people and to love God.

137

'When you give to the poor,' said Jesus, 'do not make a show of it. Give quietly, so that not even your best friend will know. But God will know, for He knows all.' Again Jesus said 'Do not pray on a street corner, or

at a place where everyone can see you. Go somewhere you can be alone.' Here is the sort of prayer which Jesus would like us to pray:

Our Father which
art in Heaven,
Hallowed be thy name.
Thy kingdom come,
Thy will be done,
On earth as it is
in Heaven.
Give us this day our
daily bread;

And forgive us our
trespasses,
As we forgive them
that trespass
against us;
And lead us not
into temptation,
But deliver us from
evil.

'Our Father in heaven;
may your holy name be honoured;
may your Kingdom come;
may your will be done on earth
   as it is in heaven.
Give us the food we need.

142

Forgive us the wrongs we have done,
  as we forgive the wrongs that others
  have done to us.
Do not bring us to hard testing,
  but keep us safe from the Evil One.'
  (Good News Bible: Matthew 6. 9-13)

143

JESUS
THE
SHEPHERD

As Jesus travelled through Palestine, he often saw sheep with their shepherds. The shepherd looked after the sheep and led them to fresh grass and water. He

used a long stick, called a staff, to lead them out of danger.

At night, he lay down in front of the sheep's pen. This kept the sheep in and the wild animals out. It was a dangerous job and the shepherd was ready to die for his sheep.

148

A good shepherd knew each of his sheep, although they might look the same to anyone else. And the sheep knew his voice and would come whenever he called them. They would not follow a stranger whose voice they did not know.

The Lost Sheep

One day Jesus told this story about a shepherd:
The shepherd had one hundred sheep. One day, as he
was counting them, he found that there were only
ninety-nine. He had lost one!

150

He did not say, 'I have ninety-nine others, I will forget the lost one.' Each one was precious to him. He could not rest until he had found the one that was missing.

So he set off, searching and calling for it. Up and down, over fields and rocks, until at last, after a long search, he found it.

The shepherd was so happy! He picked up the tired sheep, put it on his shoulders, and carried it back home to safety.

When he got back home he celebrated the good news with his friends and neighbours.

Jesus said that God was like the shepherd. Whenever anyone strays away from him by doing wrong, God

longs for that person to come back to him. When he does, there is great happiness in heaven.

Jesus said that He, Himself, is like a good shepherd too. We are like His sheep. 'I am ready to die for my sheep,' said Jesus. 'Those who are my sheep know my voice. And I want those who are not yet my sheep to come to me too.'

Jesus died on the cross for us. But He rose to life again three days later. He is greater even than death.

People from all over the world are still coming to Jesus today. Those who love Him and try to live as He asks, are His sheep.

The Lost Son

Jesus told this story about a lost boy:

There was a man who had two sons. They knew that when their father died he would leave everything to them.

But the younger son could not wait. He asked his father if he could have his share now.

158

So the father divided all he had and gave the son his share. The son sold it all and went away to a distant country. He led a wild life and wasted his money in silly ways. Soon it was all gone.

Then there was a bad famine and the boy found himself with nothing — no food, no money, no home. He knew that he must work. He found a job looking after pigs.

He was so hungry he would have eaten the pigs' food.

He was very miserable. He knew that even his father's servants had more to eat than he did. He decided to go home and ask his father if he could be a servant too.

So he started on the long trek home.

All the time he had been away, his father had longed for him to return. He kept looking at the road to see if he could see his son.

At last, one day, he saw him in the distance. How ragged and unhappy he looked! But the father knew his own son. He ran to meet him, and he hugged and kissed him.

'Father,' began the boy, 'I have done wrong — against God and against you. I am not fit to be your son. Let me be a servant ....'

But his father did not seem to hear him. He cried out to his servants, 'Hurry up! Bring him the best robe

and shoes, and a ring for his finger. Prepare a splendid feast. For my son who was lost has been found!'

We are like the young boy when we do wrong. Like the father, God is so happy when we come back to Him.

JESUS'S WONDERFUL MIRACLES

Jesus Feeds a Crowd

Lots of people loved to come and meet Jesus. Often they came to be healed or to hear him teach. Because He was the Son of God, He could do the most wonderful things.

Some days there were so many people waiting to see Him that Jesus hardly had time to eat.

On one such day, Jesus said to His disciples,
His special friends, 'Come, let us go
and find somewhere quiet where
we can be alone and rest.'
So they got into a boat and began
to row across the lake.

But many people had seen them leave and they didn't
want to lose sight of Jesus. So they ran around the
shore of the lake and reached the other side before
Jesus's boat arrived.

When He stepped out of the boat and saw the large
crowd, Jesus was not angry. Nor did he tell the
people to go away. Jesus never turns anyone away.
He felt sorry for them. Although he was tired himself,
He welcomed them and began to teach and to heal
those who were sick.

There were about five thousand men, women and
children there that day.

They stayed throughout the day and, as evening approached, the disciples told Jesus to send the people away, so that they could go to the farms and villages to get something to eat.

But Jesus told His disciples that
they should give the people
something to eat.
The disciples were puzzled by this,
for they had not enough food to
feed such a great number of people.
And there was nowhere nearby
where they might buy any.

172

'It would cost a lot of money for everyone to have even a little,' said Philip, who was one of the disciples.

Then Andrew, another of the disciples, noticed a boy in the crowd. He had brought his own meal along with him.

Andrew said to Jesus, 'There is a boy here who has five loaves and two fish – but they will certainly not be enough to feed all these people.'

But no difficulty is too great for Jesus to overcome, as the disciples were about to find out.

'Tell everyone to sit on the grass,' He said. The people sat down in groups. Then Jesus took the loaves and fish which the boy had given, and He gave thanks to God, who is the Giver of all things. He broke the loaves and gave them and the fish to the disciples, who then handed them out to the people.

174

175

As the disciples passed through the crowd they found that the food never seemed to come to an end! The five loaves and two fish were more than enough for over five thousand people. How wonderful Jesus is! When the crowd had all had enough to eat, Jesus said to His disciples, 'Now go round and gather up all that is left. We must not waste any.'

The disciples did as He asked and when they had finished, they found that they had twelve baskets full. The crowd were astonished. They had seen one of Jesus's miracles with their own eyes.

'He must be the great prophet who is to come into the world; the one we have been expecting for so long,' they said, as they went home, wondering. The young boy who had given Jesus his picnic lunch would have a wonderful true story to tell his parents when he got back home! They would all remember how Jesus had made a great deal out of a very small offering.

Jesus does this all the time. We all have gifts we can offer to Him: our time, our money, and our talents. In fact, all the things we do well — and we can all do well at something. When we offer them to Him, He can make a lot of them — just as He can make tiny grains of wheat grow into bread to feed us.

Jesus turns water into wine

One day, soon after Jesus had started His work, there was a wedding in a little village named Cana. Jesus was invited and so was His mother. So too were Jesus's special friends who were called His disciples.

At the wedding, everyone gave their good wishes to the man and woman who were being married, and they all drank wine made from grapes. It was a very happy time and the people enjoyed it.

Then suddenly, the servants realised that they did not have enough wine. What could they do? They did not want to tell the people that their master had not supplied enough. He would have been very upset.

Jesus's mother, Mary, noticed how worried
they were; so she said quietly to Jesus,
'They have no wine left.' Mary did
not know what Jesus could do
about it, but she felt sure
He would help in some
way, as He had often

done before. Jesus will always help us, if we ask Him
and really trust Him to do what He knows is best.
So Mary said to the servants,
'Do whatever He tells you.'
Nearby, there were six stone jars which were
used to hold water. They were huge jars, each one
held about one hundred litres.

'Fill those jars with water,' said Jesus.
The servants filled the jars up to the brim. Then Jesus said,
'Now pour some out and take it to the man who is in charge
of the party.' The servants did so.
The man in charge could not understand what was

happening. He tasted the drink which the servants brought to him and found that it was not water, as he expected, but wine! It was very good wine too.
He had no idea where it could have come from — but the servants knew that it was because of what Jesus had done.

The man in charge asked the bridegroom (the man who had just been married) to come to him and said, 'This is wonderful wine. Your party is different. Most people serve the best wine first, and when everyone has had some, then they serve more ordinary wine. But you have done it the other way. You have kept the best wine until last!'

Neither the bridegroom nor the man in charge knew that it was Jesus who had saved the party – though perhaps they found out afterwards.

186

When Jesus does something wonderful like this, which ordinary people cannot do, it is called a miracle.

The wedding at Cana was Jesus's first miracle; when His disciples saw it, they knew that Jesus had come to bring joy to God's people. It shows us how Jesus is interested in everything which happens to us — our work, our families, our friends, our play — and our parties.